5s for Supervisors

By Ade Asefeso MCIPS MBA

Second Edition

ISBN-13: 978-1499637250

ISBN-10: 149963725X

Publisher: AA Global Sourcing Ltd
Website: http://www.aaglobalsourcing.com

Table of Contents

Disclaimer

This publication is designed to provide competent and reliable information regarding the subject matter covered. However, it is sold with the understanding that the author and publisher are not engaged in rendering professional advice. The authors and publishers specifically disclaim any liability that is incurred from the use or application of contents of this book.

Dedication

This book is dedicated to the hundreds of thousands of incredible souls in the world who have weathered through the up and down of recent recession.

To my good friend and mentor Andy Hobbs who seems to have been sent here to teach me something about who I am supposed to be. He has nurtured me and my son Karl, challenged me, and even opposed me…. But at every juncture has taught me!

This book is dedicated to my lovely boys, Thomas, Michael and Karl. Teaching them to manage their finance will give them the lives they deserve. They have taught me more about life, presence, and energy management than anything I have done in my life.

Chapter 1: Introduction

5S is a set of techniques providing a standard approach to housekeeping within Lean Manufacturing. It is often promoted as being far more than simply housekeeping and some of the elements described below certainly have broader implications.

It originated, as did most of the elements of JIT (Just in Time), within Toyota. A cornerstone of 5S is that untidy, cluttered work areas are not productive. As well as the physical implications of junk getting in everybody's way and dirt compromising quality, we are all happier in a clean and tidy environment and hence more inclined to work hard and with due care and attention.

Naturally enough, the elements of 5S are all Japanese words beginning with the letter S. Since their adoption within Western implementations of JIT, or Lean Manufacturing, various anglicised versions of the terms have been adopted by different writers and educators. These are listed below against the individual elements and it can be seen that none are entirely satisfactory.

Seiri (Sort)

Seiri is the identification of the best physical Organisation of the workplace. It has been variously anglicised as Sort, Systematisation or Simplify by those wishing to retain the S as the initial letter of each element. It is the series of steps by which we identify things which are being held in the workplace when they shouldn't, or are being held in the wrong place.

Put simply, we may identify a large area devoted to tools or gauges, some of which are needed regularly and some used infrequently. This brings all sorts of problems, including:

1. Operators unable to find the item they need. The time spent searching is a waste (or in Japanese speak a muda) and if we only held the items needed regularly in a prominent position we would save time.
2. Quality issues when gauges are not calibrated on time because too many are held.
3. Safety issues when people fall over things.
4. Lockers and racking cluttering the workplace making it hard to move around or to see each other and communicate.

Some of the standard texts also talk about the elimination of excess materials and WIP. This is a complete restatement of all the JIT goals of releasing capital, reduced movement, shorter cycle times and so on. The question may be asked; should we then see inventory and WIP reduction as part of the implementation of the lean approach or as an element of 5S?

The answer, as ever, is that keeping inventory and WIP to a minimum is simple best practice. Whether we view it as JIT, or lean, or 5S or assign any other term is quite frankly irrelevant.

The major element of Seiri is simply a critical look at the area. Involving cross-functional teams, or looking at each other's areas, is an obvious first step. People tend to be blind to failings in their own work place and a fresh pair of eyes can be useful.

Another element of the standard approach is 'red tagging' where items are given a tag which says what the item is, which location it is in and when it was identified in this location. We then leave the area for a while and anybody using the item notes this. We go back some time later and can readily identify things that haven't moved, or been used. Items which have not been used can then potentially be disposed of. As a first pass we should perhaps create a quarantine area before throwing items away, selling them or reworking them into something else.

Other items may be deemed necessary but used infrequently and so an alternative location can be found. If the operator needs a particular tool only once or twice a month then a 20-yard walk is not a problem especially if the space thus saved on the workbench helps to make the workplace more productive, or helps address quality issues.

Seiton (Set)

Seiton is the series of steps by which the optimum organisation identified in the sort are put into place. The standard translation is Orderliness but again some wish to keep the initial S and use Sort (yes, that is also one of the translations of Seiri), Set in order, Straighten and Standardisation.

The sorting out process is essentially a continuation of that described in the Seiri phase. Removing items to be discarded or held in an alternative location will create space. This space will be visible and facilitate the alternative layout of the area. In some cases, of course, we are talking about what a fitter will have on his bench, or in racks alongside the bench. In other cases we may be considering where we should locate a piece of plant; for example we may relocate a coin press to enable items to be completed in one work area rather than requiring a significant movement down the shop.

This is something which we also undertake when adopting cellular manufacturing. We then look at how we can restructure the work content so that certain operations can be carried out within the cycle of others; for example we may carry out a trimming operation on a steel component while the press which produced it is busy creating the next one. Again, is this a 5S initiative, or part of a kaizen programme, or something else?

Again, who cares, as long as we get on and achieve an improvement in business performance?

Standardisation includes all the elements of setting out a consistent way of doing things. This includes standard manufacturing methodologies, standard equipment and tooling, component rationalisation, drawing standardisation, consistency in the documentation which accompanies work, design for manufacture (or concurrent engineering) and standardisation in the clerical processes which deliver work to the shop floor and track its progress.

All of this could be said to be part of a basic Total Quality approach. The standard ways of doing things should include poka-yoke or error-proofing. Again it might be asked whether this is part of 5S or one aspect of a broader programme.

Seiso (Shine)

Anglicised as Cleanliness but again the initial S can be retained in Shine, or Sweeping. The principle here is that we are all happier and hence more productive in clean, bright environments. There is a more practical element in that if everything is clean it is immediately ready for use. We would not want a precision product to be adjusted by a spanner that is covered in grease which may get into some pneumatic or hydraulic fittings. We would not wish to compromise a PCB assembly by metallic dust picked up from an unclean work surface.

Other issues are health and safety (perhaps slipping in a puddle of oil, shavings blowing into people's eyes) and machine tools damaged by coolant contaminated by grease and dust.

The task is to establish the maintenance of a clean environment as an ongoing, continuous programme. Some time should be set aside for cleaning each day, or each shift. (We may have cleaners who come in a sweep office floors, and even clean the floor in a production area, but they do not clean the production equipment. Even if they did, this would miss one of the opportunities available an operator cleaning and lubricating his machine tool will spot worn or damaged components.) Cleaning then begins to impinge upon what we already know as preventive maintenance. Cleaning critical components of a piece of equipment is already one element of the activities carried out under the preventive maintenance banner.

The implementation of Seiso revolves around two main elements.
1. The first is the assignment map which identifies who is responsible for which areas.
2. The second is the schedule which says who does what at which times and on which days.

Some of these happen before a shift begins, some during the shift and some at the end. Again, this is very reminiscent of what we do when adopting preventive maintenance.

The standard texts such as that of Hiroyuki Hirano then go on to talk about establishing the shine method for each item / area. This includes such elements as agreeing an inspection step at the beginning of each shift, establishing exactly how each activity within the programme is to be carried out. A key aspect is very much akin to set-up reduction (or SMED) in that we should be aiming as much as possible to internalise the activities in other words, to minimise the downtime needed to keep the facilities clean.

Finally the standard texts talk about preparation making sure the equipment needed to clean is always available, always ready for use. The best parallel to this is, again, with set-up reduction, which itself is often compared to Grand Prix teams preparing to change tyres. As with many such topics, we are talking about here is to a large extent simply common sense. We do not wish to allocate 5 minutes for a bed to be swept on a piece of grinding equipment if the operator is going to spend 4 minutes finding his brush.

Seiketsu (Standardisation)

This is best described as Standardised cleanup, but other names adopted include Standardisation (not to be confused with the second "S"set), Systematisation and Sanitation.

Seiketsu can be the thought of as the means by which we maintain the first S. There is, obviously, a danger in any improvement activity that once the focus is removed and another 'hot button' grabs management attention, things go back to the way they were before. Seiketsu is the set of techniques adopted to prevent this happening. Basically this involves setting a schedule by which all the elements are revisited on a regular basis; usually referred to as the '5S Job Cycle.'

The first step in the cycle is a periodic review of the area, perhaps involving red tagging but certainly involving people from other areas of the business. This will identify where standards have slipped; for example where pieces of tooling or fixtures which are used infrequently are no longer being put in the remote location agreed at the outset and consequently a bench is now cluttered with the regular items buried under a pile of irregular. (In other words, the Seiri phase is undertaken periodically; usually monthly, perhaps quarterly.)

The second step is to undertake Seiton activities as required that is, as prompted by the first step.

Finally within Seiketsu people from other areas visit and cast a critical eye over the state of the area. Again, an external assessor may notice degradation that is not clear to the people who work in the area. Hirano talks of a checklist within Seiketsu whereby the external visitors mark the area on a number of key criteria defined at the outset of the programme. For example, are the storage areas still clearly defined? Does the tool rack still have clear outlines or profiles for each tool?

Shitsuke (Sustain)

The final stage is that of Discipline. For those who wish to retain the use of initial S's in English this is often listed as Sustain or Self-discipline. There is a fundamental difference between Seiketsu and Shitsuke.

The fourth "S" Standardisation is the introduction of a formal, rigorous review programme to ensure that the benefits of the approach are maintained.

The fifth "S" is more than this; it is not simply the mechanical means by which we continue to monitor and refine, it is the set of approaches we use to win hearts and minds, to make people want to keep applying best practice in shop organisation and housekeeping. In this sense, discipline is perhaps an unfortunate term as it implies people forced to do something, with consequent penalties if they do not.

The way in which management achieves this establishment of ongoing commitment within the workforce depends, of course, on the culture already in place. As with the adoption of kaizen (continuous improvement) or quality circles we have to press the right buttons to stimulate people. If the business has a history of treating people like cattle, giving no credence to their suggestions and simply trying to improve performance by driving the workers ever harder, then enthusiasm for any sort of initiative aimed at building a better environment is going to be hard to generate.

There are a number of elements to any ongoing improvement activity in any business. Which take pre-eminence in a particular organisation varies with the history and culture of that organisation.

Suffice to say that key points are:
1. Communication: We need people to be aware of what we are trying to achieve, and why.
2. Education: They need to understand the concepts and the individual techniques.
3. Rewards and Recognition: People need to feel that their efforts are recognised. Whether the

reward is a senior manager walking past and saying "that's very good, well done" or some form of award (financial gain, prize or formal presentation of a certificate) depends on the organisation.

4. Time: If we want people to spend five minutes every four hours removing swarf from the floor around their machine we have to make sure that we allow them this time. We cannot give this as an instruction yet at the same time push for more time spent achieving productivity targets.

5. Structure: We need to identify what is to be done, by whom, and ensure that schedules are updated and clearly visible.

Implementing 5S

Would we want to launch 5S as a stand-alone project, as a complete entity?

The elements of 5S are all valuable in their own right but they simply form part of the bigger picture of establishing best practice. They sit alongside the other elements of Lean Manufacturing, or Just in Time, or World Class and some of the elements in, for example, Seiton (standardisation) are in fact straight lifts from textbooks on other forms of improvement activity. There is nothing in any 5S material, for example, to give guidance on improving the clerical processes for generating production paperwork following receipt of a sales order!

The answer, surely, is to understand 5S as we understand all aspects of other types of improvement and problem-solving activity and then to agree a change programme for our own business. This is not to say that we must not launch a project which we call "5S" some businesses have more success if improvement initiatives are launched with a generic, well-publicised term as project name. Equally, this is not the best solution in other organisations. Again, the history and culture of the company or the specific plant have to be taken into account when this decision is taken.

Chapter 2: Is Your Company Culture Ready for Lean Thinking?

With all of the workshops, books, web pages, and presentations that have been made available over the past few years on the topic of lean improvement, one would think that a high percentage of our organizations would be a lot leaner by now. Unfortunately, I don't believe that is the case. Sure, some companies have made significant progress, and many more have implemented a few significant improvement projects, but has the majority of the group really installed a sustainable set of lean approaches?

I have lived through the fads of quality circles, total quality management, and re-engineering. I now strongly suspect that I will witness the same rise and fall of enthusiasm for the six sigma and lean enterprise methodologies in the next year or so. It's not that I am a cynic as much as I feel that the same systemic factors exist to drag these improvement initiatives down. You might say that it has become our business improvement culture to get excited about a seemingly new way to save time and money, spend a lot of resources trying to learn and use the new tools, and still slowly watch the interest fade over time. In turn, it is only fitting that the source of such demise lies in a failure to change our cultures to support these new ways of thinking and acting each day.

Most improvement efforts fail because we try to impose the tools that best define them upon a culture that in most cases is not really ready for their use. Improvement gurus will tell you right off the bat that a culture change is necessary for sustained success, but only a select few of them will give you a clear picture of the types of changes that are really needed to make such a culture change occur. If they were brutally honest, it would be a lot harder to sell the new tools, workshops, and books, because we are culturally conditioned to seek instant gratification; the quick fix. Culture change can happen quickly, but the degree and types of personal change required, especially at the leadership level, is enough to disenchant an executive more quickly than a clear, sunny day entices them to head for the golf course.

Our culture is the foundation for our daily behaviours, and in turn, our daily results. Culture can be simply defined by looking at the collective set of behaviours that we display on the job each day; how we make decisions, how we treat people, how we react to problems, how we dress, and how we decorate our work areas. A given work culture has existed as long as its facility, and to a lesser degree its organization, has. It is a product of past history, the belief systems of the people it has hired, and the external environment it co-exists with. It is foolhardy to expect significant change to happen simply by asking people to do their jobs differently, sending them to classes that expose them to new tools, or issuing a group e-mail of new job expectations.

Think about it. To begin with, our social culture is more powerful than our work culture. It is not a cultural attribute of Americans or European to be lean. Sure, we might say that we want to be lean, but the recent statistics on obesity seem to contradict such statements. In most cases, the cultural angles that we pursue to make our companies leaner are analogous to the repeated purchases we make for machines that will firm up our abs; we buy the tools, but we fail to make them part of our daily lives. After awhile, they find their eternal resting place in our closets. Hopefully, we bought the collapsible variety so storage is not too much of a problem.

Our company cultures are reshaping themselves each day, but this shaping is also always occurring around a core culture. The culture loop shown on the right is a reinforcing one; our culture shapes our beliefs about how things are done or should be done, our beliefs drive our on the job behaviours, our behaviours lead us to create the systems we consciously or unconsciously use at work, and our systems help shape and reinforce the culture that is in place. There is both promise and peril in this loop. If it is understood and appreciated, we can use systems change as a mechanism to help shift our culture more quickly and to a greater degree. If we take the loop for granted or ignore it, the culture loop can spin us into complacency, or worse yet, business failure.

Henry Ford once said "If you always do what you've always done, you'll always get what you've always gotten." This quote reflects the influence of culture, and while many of us might recognize it, fewer of us embrace its true message. If you want your lean initiative to survive, much less thrive, you have to change your existing work systems and behaviours to support it. Asking people to change or mandating that they attend classes or pass certification tests alone won't do it. In most cases, an existing work culture will even prevent the use of tools by an experienced practitioner (one who had repeatedly practiced tool use as opposed to merely being exposed to how they are supposed to work). If you want instant gratification, you better make some significant systems changes.

While the cultural norm for merely pontificating in this book without giving you any real substance is tempting, I would really like to see us move away from the fad chasing behaviours that we tend to exhibit as a culture, so I had better offer you some tangible system changes that my experience has shown really make a difference. Here are the top ten ways to help make your lean initiative survive and thrive:

1. Redesign the jobs of all people, and in particular all supervisors and managers, to include significant time for work on lean improvement projects; don't simply ask them to do more with less.

2. Install a bottom-up system for measuring the degree to which your managers and supervisors consistently practice lean behaviours on the job; don't simply expect them to adopt these new behaviours on their own.

3. Redesign all training sessions to minimize the use of lecture and maximize the amount of training time that is spent on skill practice; don't continue to rely primarily on lecture as a means of helping people learn.
4. Compensate people in a manner that is fair, equitable, and commensurate with the level of lean improvements that they make; don't lay them off as improvements are made.
5. Define a balanced set of performance measures for all key work processes and visually trend performance over time; don't limit your measurement efforts to the production lines and tables of numbers on paper.
6. Regularly involve your internal and external customers in your lean improvement projects and learning events; don't ignore your internal customers and only talk to your external ones when they have problems or when you want more from them.
7. Use technology to make all daily tasks leaner and to share lean success information across the company; don't remain stuck in an analogue mindset and limit communication to bad news or changes that have to be made.
8. Identify waste streams and their daily costs for all key work processes, and work to minimize these streams over time; don't assume that any process is waste free.
9. Build lean improvement projects into the overall site improvement plan and be cognizant of all project resource needs (time

and money) don't keep them on a separate project list or fail to keep a list at all.

10. Measure the cost and effectiveness of all group events, and work to drive costs down and effectiveness up over time; don't meet for an hour on every Monday just because you always have in the past.

I wish that I could say that these improvement ideas came to me in a dream, but in reality, I learned them from personal success and failure over the years and through my 25 years experience in corporate world. They don't represent the way that typical companies do business each day, but they are typical of systems that support the sustained, excellent results that high performance workplaces get each day. If you only choose to try using a few of them, I can guarantee that your probability of lean initiative success will be greatly enhanced.

Systems shape culture, and without culture change, your lean initiative will end up resembling the total quality management effort that your company tried twenty years ago. I wish this wasn't true, but I have seen too many attempts to lose weight, reduce credit card debt, and exercise more go by the wayside. Our existing culture encourages us to buy the tools and attend the classes, and the rest will take of itself. That however is not the cultural attitude that the high performing companies take.

Chapter 3: 10 Things an Operations Supervisor Can Do Today to Improve Reliability

If you are new to the position of Operations Supervisor, what are some of the things you can begin working on immediately to improve reliability within the area you work?

1. **Learn Your Process:** The first thing someone is going to tell you on the day someone touches you on the forehead and appoints you an Operations Supervisor is; "you don't need to learn how the equipment works or how the product is made, you just need to learn how to manage people." Take it from someone who has been there, that is a bunch of bull crap. Something tells me that Steve Jobs and Bill Gates have a very good idea what it takes to make a computer and write software, and in the early days of their respective companies, they both had to supervise people. In this new job, you will be expected to make decisions that will impact the products you make and the customers they are sold to, so your first priority should be to learn the process and learn it well. Lean on your most experienced operators to show you the ropes and start going through production data as well as failure history.

2. **Follow Procedures:** Having cut my teeth in different industries, our equipment operators had a procedure or checklist for nearly everything they did. We had procedures on how to start the equipment

up, how to shut it down, and how to change products. I was surprised when I went into the consulting business to find out that most companies have very few Standard Operating Procedures (SOP). They instead rely on each operator to start equipment and run products based on memory or experience. If something goes wrong in the process, they eat the loss and then identify it as a training opportunity or learning experience. The reality is that as an Operations Supervisor you need the equipment to run consistently each and every shift and the only way to deliver consistent operations is for two things to be true and consistent. The first is to have SOPs and Operator Checklists. If your department does not have these procedures and checklists in place, now is the time to get it done. The second thing is that your equipment must be reliable.

3. Review/Audit Procedures: Now that you have procedures in place, you and your operators need to review and audit them. Reviewing procedures gets people who have experience involved using a continuous improvement model to develop the best procedures. Audits are necessary to ensure the operators are in fact using the SOPs and checklists on a daily basis. Reinforce the people who are using the procedures and those who are actively involved in improving procedures.

4. Know Process Performance Standards: Being new to this job, you may not even know what this means. Process performance standards are things like line rate for a given product, the quality standards you need to maintain for the product (including how it's packaged), and the health, safety, and environmental standards you are held to in manufacturing that product. Why is this important? As our equipment is in the process of failing, it typically fails to deliver on one or more performance standards before it completely stops. This is known as functional failure. If your packaging machine is supposed to produce 325 packages of good quality product per minute and it is making any amount less than this, it has functionally failed. In understanding your performance standards, you can begin looking for what has failed, or what is in the process of failing before the equipment actually stops. Once the equipment stops, if you have no idea what caused the rate to drop off, you will be left to guess on what needs to be repaired. Performance standards when properly maintained allow us to effectively plan and schedule both production and maintenance activities.

5. Understand Equipment Criticality (Logic-Based Decisions): As I stated earlier, you will be making decisions that will impact the product you make and the customers who use that product. As a result, you need to make sound, logic-based decisions and these decisions become much easier if you understand the criticality of your assets. While this exercise is often driven and seen as a maintenance tool, it is in fact a tool everyone at your company can use to help make sound decisions if done properly. Two pieces of advice here; if your company has not performed an asset criticality assessment, you need to get that started right away; if they have performed one in the past, take a random sample of 100 assets, chart the criticality ranking of each, and make sure the distribution is also random. If the data is normal, left or right skewed, the assessment was flawed and needs to be done again.

6. Be Customer/Product Focused: Reliability is a broad subject, but when it comes down to it, our customers help us to define reliability. Customers set product demand and product demand sets our desired performance standards for both rate and quality. Your job, simply put, is to make high quality products and meet customer demand. But, using 25 years of experience, I can tell you that you will be insulated from your customer and the feedback you get from them will be second or third hand. If you want your process to run in a smooth and reliable fashion, YOU need to know your customers. Just one example I can share comes from a site I visited last year. They had just finished a 6-day, 100,000 piece order of good quality product; however, the problem was that the product was not packaged correctly on the pallets and it all had to be taken apart and restacked. This took 5 full days to complete and the customer's order was late. Had the Operations Supervisors known the customer, they would have also known how the customer wanted the order stacked.

7. Reinforce the Right Behaviours: This is where learning how to lead people comes into play. I can also tell you that in your very first week, you will be confronted with some problems you'll have no idea how to resolve.

8. Learn/Understand Product data management (PDM): Yes, as an Operations Supervisor you need to learn and understand a handful of predictive technologies, including Airborne Ultrasound, Infrared Thermography, Vibration Analysis, and Lubrication Analysis. If you fail to understand the technologies and how they are applied to detect potential failures, you will make emotional decisions instead of fact-based decisions. While this might be the most difficult undertaking of the items on this list, have faith that having this skill set on your resume will go a long way regardless of the career path you decide to take.

9. RCA – Learn It, Set Triggers, and Implement: Root Cause Analysis (RCA) should be the Operations Supervisor's best friend. A good RCA process is going to help you eliminate failures in every aspect of your business. When I say learn Root Cause Analysis, what I mean is that you need to learn what works for you and use it. There are a variety of problem solving tools out there, from Ishikawa Diagrams to Cause Mapping; the trick here is to have a group of people who have learned each and specialize in at least one. Once you and your people have been trained, it's time to set triggers for when you need to perform an RCA, and once you have begun performing them, you need to implement the mitigating tasks. An important thing to remember, rarely is there one "Root Cause"; realistically, there are often several. As a result, remember to save your information just in case the problem comes back. As someone who has made a living at helping people and companies solve problems, the best facilitators don't tell you what they think your problems are, they instead teach you how to identify and eliminate them. When you find a great instructor or facilitator, insist that they instruct and facilitate all critical RCAs.

10. Keep It Clean: If I can make a general statement, clean equipment is more reliable than dirty equipment. I see it every day and have countless examples of how dirt, dust, and clutter have a detrimental impact on the reliability of manufacturing equipment. As an Operations Supervisor, you will set the bar for what clean means. If you set it too low, you should expect a greater number of random and wear-based failures. Set it too high and you may sacrifice some time where the equipment could have been making product. The trick here is to do as much as you can in about 20 minutes, and write an SOP for the cleanup required in each area. There are some great tools out there for developing good cleaning practices, including Operator Care, Total Productive Maintenance (TPM), 5S, and Kaizen. Take your pick and get it done!

So there you have it! Congratulations on becoming an Operations Supervisor. Some of the best CEOs in the world started their career with this critical step, and well, some of the worst CEOs must have skipped it all together because this position, regardless of what others might say, impacts company performance more than any other. Time to step up and lead!

Chapter 4: How to Start 5S Program

One important purpose and benefit of 5S or 6S is to make your work area clean and in order to unhide potential problems. In an unclean workplace, it is hard to even notice things like "When did that machine start making that noise?" or "When did that start leaking oil?"

Another purpose and benefit is to reduce the amount of time wasted looking for misplaced tools, and materials, and supplies.

Most Lean initiatives start out with 5S training as one of the earliest initiatives, and there is a flurry of enthusiastic cleaning and organizing. The real test, however, is how well the new ways "stick" over time. The success of your 5s program is often an excellent predictor of the probable success of your greater lean manufacturing initiative.

Training is always the first step. And because 5S is often the first introduction to the entire concept of Lean continuous improvement; patient attention should be given to ensure that people's fears, misconceptions, and questions are fully answered. Most importantly, management must convincingly lay to rest the fear of "improving ourselves out of a job." (How?)

After initial 5S training, every lean leader has their own favourite way of implementing an initial workspace clean up.

The essential thing is to have the workers evaluate every tool and machine, every pile of materials and supplies, every piece of instructional paper... to decide what is actually used, and how often.

This can be done by marking any suspect items with a red tag, and then moving it out of the area into a temporary holding area (just in case it really is needed)...

It can be accomplished by holding a mock auction; where the workers "bid" to plead their case for why an item should be kept.

The end result is to Sort the useful from the clutter.

Depending on the volume and complexity of the initial clutter; Sort can be its own phase, or you might have time to move right into an initial round of Set and Shine.

Remember to take before and after photos and distribute your highly visual success story far and wide to begin generating enthusiasm for your Lean program.

Once you have "picked the low-hanging fruit" of the first 3 phases of 5S, you will soon be challenged with the tough ones...

The 4th and 5th S's are by far the most important...
Standardize and Sustain. Your success or failure with
Standard Work will determine the success or failure
of your entire lean program.

There is really no sense in even beginning a new
flavour-of-the-month   initiative   if   your   top
management is not sincerely committed to seeing this
through for long-term cultural transformation. And to
do THAT... you are going to need to look ahead at
the 2 tough S's...

You are going to need a wide variety of diverse
templates, training, and systems to empower your
people with the right tools and methods to improve a
wide variety of diverse types of processes.

5S is not (successfully) implemented in isolation. The
Shingo Prize teachings make it clear...

The typical Lean Journey usually starts with using one
lean tool to solve one isolated problem (5S is a
common starting point)   and then (If that initial
small project is successful)... the usual, expected, and
desired path is to become exposed to (and competent
with) many other lean tools and methods eventually
evolving into integrated synergistic lean systems.

Chapter 5: Top 10 Tips for 5s Success

There are a lot of benefits to be gained by putting a 5S process in place, but many organizations fail to successfully accomplish this goal. The following ten suggestions are intended to help you avoid the failures that others have suffered as you attempt to make your workplace more sorted, set in order, shine, standardized, and self-disciplined.

1. Don't See Your 5S Initiative as a Stand Alone Effort: Besides bringing up 'program of the month' memories from the past amongst your people, treating your 5S initiative as a standalone process will create a lot of confusion about why you are undertaking this effort and will result in the inefficient use of resources. Many companies use special training, audits, and meetings that have a specific 5S focus in an effort to get the program going. Instead, you should build 5S practices and expectations into your larger performance improvement plan and operational excellence strategies. Similarly, don't form a 5S specific team instead; build 5S initiative reviews into your regular Leadership Team and workgroup team meetings.

2. Require Management to Set a Strong 5S Example: Nothing will kill a 5S effort quicker than having employees walk by messy managers' desks or work areas right after they have attended a 5S project update meeting. Just as the Leadership Team should be the most effective team in a given company, the work areas of managers in a 5S company should be the cleanest and most organized. Additionally, you should expect every member of management to support 5S practices consistently and regularly if a manager sees someone not practicing 5S ideals, they should politely challenge those people and ask them to correct the behaviour or condition, even if that person does not report to them.

3. Require Every Supervisor and Manager to Enforce 5S Practices on a Daily Basis: The monthly walk through (high performance workplace audit) discussed below serves as a great tool for providing measurable 5S progress and for reinforcing the ultimate in 5S expectations, but you should also recognize that supervisors are conducting performance audits whenever they are out there with their people. What is not said often sends a stronger message than what is said; if a supervisor walks by someone who is violating a 5S (or other type of high performance) expectation and does not say anything, they are telling that employee that their behaviour is okay. Similarly, the daily reinforcement of good 5S practices when they are exhibited carries much more weight than saying 'thank you' to the overall group in a meeting.

4. Incorporate 5S Expectations into EVERY Employee's Job Description: If you want your work areas to remain sorted, set in order, and shiny, expect each employee to leave them that way when they go home for the evening. This is best accomplished by (1) rewriting EVERY job description to include this expectation, (2) emphasizing this expectation in work group meetings, and (3) providing immediate performance feedback when a workplace does not meet the expectation at the end of a shift or day.

5. Clearly, and Visually, Define What Each 5S Workplace Should Look Like: 'before and after' pictures of 5S progress send a strong message about what is expected and will be recognized. Pictures also help people better understand what each 5S concept will look like when it is actually put in place on the job. You may also benefit from taking your work groups over to a '5S best practice' work area and talking about the differences between that workplace and how their own currently looks.

6. Modify Procedures and Work Instructions to Keep 5S Changes Alive: If you want all of your people to adhere to the "A place for everything and everything in its place" philosophy, you had better rewrite your procedures to include steps for putting things back where they belong. You also need to make sure that clear, easy to use procedures exist for disposing of waste or obsolete product or supplies. After all, don't our work instructions define what we are expected to do at work each day?

7. Build 5S Expectations Into Your Monthly High Performance Work Practices Walk-Through: Sure, you can do a special 5S walk-through each month just like you do the monthly safety inspection, but your time will be much better invested if you create a monthly high performance practices walk through assessment tool and include 5S expectations as part of it. For example, in addition to looking for consistency of 5S practices, also look for consistency in the use of visual performance postings, safe work practices, proper lean changeovers, six sigma project support, and employee awareness of high performance concepts as you move through each workplace.

8. Include 5S Recognition in Your Regular Employee Recognition Efforts: The best thing you can do is recognize each team each month that meets or exceeds the minimum score on the high performance work practices walk through. Avoid the tendency to give out a "Cleanest Workplace of the Month" or a "Most Organized Department" award, and especially avoid punishing people for being 'one of the worst'. You only have so many recognition dollars/pounds to spend in your budget; use them to recognize team success against an all encompassing set of high performance work practice criteria.

9. Create a 5S Punch List and Show Regular Progress Towards Its Completion: One of the best things about putting 5S in place is that once you get over the initial hump, it is relatively easy to keep 5S alive. For example, once you have sorted out all of your obsolete equipment and supplies, you should not have to do those tasks again as long as your people each fulfil the expectations of their 'modified' daily job. By creating a single 5S punch list for the whole facility, reviewing it weekly as part of your Leadership Team meeting (don't form a 5S Implementation Team), and tracking the percent complete for each action item on the action plan, you can easily keep up with the progress of your initiative.

10. Create a 5S Implementation Plan with Milestones that Appreciate Process Evolution: If you follow the above nine guidelines, you should see progress in a relatively short amount of time. Additionally, you should see little regression back to where you were when you started your 5S initiative. For example, after 3-6 weeks of consistent sweeping and straightening up at the end of each day, that behaviour should have become a habit, each workplace should be much cleaner, and the need to emphasize and spend time on these two pieces of the 5S puzzle should be low. Also, once you have undertaken that big effort to get rid of all of the stuff you have collected over the years and created a reorganized approach to storage in all work areas, you should not have to worry about doing those tasks again.

Finally, I hope you can see how other operational excellence and lean six sigma approaches can benefit from using several of these approaches as well. For example, if you are going to change job descriptions to include a 5S emphasis, consider including six sigma project support and process improvement tool practice in those changes as well. In short, build high performance practices, expectations, and measurements into the larger work systems.

Chapter 6: 5s Best Practices

5S is a workplace organization methodology named after five Japanese words "seiri," "seiton," "seiso," "seiketsu" and "shitsuke," translating to "sort," "set in order," "shine," "standardize," and "sustain." 5S best practices ensure productivity, quality, and safety improvement.

5S Best Practices Related to Seri (Sort)

The first 5S principle is Seri or "Sort" that advocates elimination of unnecessary tools, parts, and instructions by retaining only the essential items.

Some established 5S best practices in this area include:

1. Red-tagging items not used, quarantining all such unnecessary items into one area, and disposing any items if they are not required for a period of one month. Chances are that an item not required for a month of smooth operations is not required in the first place.
2. Establishing wastebaskets within four steps of an employee to encourage throwing away junk as the junk is created.
3. Not allowing unnecessary items such as family pictures, post it notes, and other non-essentials posted on walls to keep walls free except for printed work related items.

Application of the 5S Sort principles bring forth many benefits such as more space, better employee communications, and easier arrangement of tools.

5S Best Practices Related to Seiton (Set in Order)

The second of 5S principles is Seiton, which means "Set in Order" or "Simplifying." This principle advocates that there should be a place for everything and everything should be in its place. All work items should be set in clearly labelled established areas and arranged in a manner that promotes efficient work flow.

Some 5S best practices in this area include:

1. Creating a 5S map of the department that shows location of all work stations, and storage areas of all tools and equipment.
2. Using labels extensively to mark item storage areas, and outlining a tools diagram on boards.
3. Using pegboards to hold the tools.
4. Using low level boxes for items held in drawers.
5. Keeping rarely used items outside the work area and using a check out sheet to log the in/out status of such tools.
6. Using visual controls to identify the location of the items. For instance, a blue tape could indicate "store here," a red tape could indicate "do not move" and so on.

5S Best Practices Related to Seiso (Shine)

Seiso, meaning "Shine" or "Cleanliness" entails keeping the workplace tidy and organized by ingraining such habits as part of the work culture instead of making cleaning a periodic exercise.

5S Best practices toward this direction include:
1. Cleaning the work area including equipments, floors, tables and cabinets, and making sure everything is restored to its place at the end of each shift using a checklist.
2. Using a portable shine cart to store cleaning supplies and moving the cart from location to location during the cleaning activity.
3. Documenting the specific procedure of cleaning required for each item to train the employees appropriately.
4. Routine scheduling of painting and other non-daily maintenance activities.
5. Keeping the workplace clean improves safety and productivity, and impresses customers.

5S Best Practices Related to Seiketsu (Standardization)

5S "Standardization" or the Seiketsu principle of 5S, establishes consistent work practices through rules and regulations in order for everyone know their exact responsibilities. This entails establishing the 5S best practices of Seri, Seiton and Seiso as the norm in the workplace.

5S Best practices in this regard include:

1. Setting a location, maintenance check schedule, cleaning procedure, and updating 5S maps whenever a new item enters the unit.
2. Conducting regular training to refresh the employees regarding 5S knowledge and responsibilities.
3. Creating a visual 5S Assessment chart that lists all the 5S tasks to be completed in a designated area, the frequency of the task, the person responsible for completing the task, and the tools needed for each task. Sorting this list in the order of the person, task, frequency, and tools, all in alphabetic order makes it easy for each person to find their own tasks and do what is required.
4. Empowering workers to participate in the development of standards.

5S Best Practices Related to Shitsuke (Sustain)

The Shitsuke or "Sustain" principle of 5S is the maintenance and review of the first four standards. The responsibility is on management to maintain focus on the 5S principles to make them a part of the work culture and not allow a gradual decline to the old ways, after the initial zeal of the 5S implementation wanes off.

5S best practices in this regard include:

1. Conducting periodic 5S audits that check not just compliance with 5S principles but the level of knowledge and awareness of employees regarding 5S stipulations.

2. Developing a checklist for the periodic audit that incorporates all the 5S practices adopted by the unit.
3. Making sure team leaders use the audit as a means to help employees through comments rather than convert the audit as a report card on 5S compliance.
4. Encouraging employees by empowering them to find better ways to sort, set, shine and standardize.
5. Developing a system of division of 5S tasks by team members themselves rather than team leaders assigning tasks.
6. Creating a system of the employee signing off the completion of each task in the 5S assessment chart, and having team leaders review the same.

5S, in its core basic, utilizes common sense that many organizations may fail to apply when first using the methodology. 5S implementation in an organization brings about improved profitability, better service and safety standards, and improves efficiency

Chapter 7: Three Important Points for Managing a 5s Process

This chapter will discuss the concept of the 5S process, its benefits, and the important points for implementing the 5S process in your company or organization.

What is the 5S Process?

The 5S process is based on five simple Japanese action words described in previous chapter as:

1. Seiri (means Sorting in English): Sort out the necessary tools, materials and discard the unnecessary items.
2. Seiton (means Set in order in English): It actually means keeping the items in such a fashion that the least human effort is required (i.e. ergonomic) to find it in the desired moment.
3. Seiso (means Cleanliness in English): Keeping the work place and the work items clean should be the daily practice rather than an occasional event.
4. Shiketsu (means Standardizing in English): Everybody should be well aware of his/her roles for maintaining the above 3S of the 5S process. The responsibility should be well defined and standard.
5. Shitsuke (means Discipline in English): After implementing the previous 4S, have

the discipline to keep on this path and not gradually revert to old methods.

The 5S is much more than a workplace organizing method. If applied properly for managing any project, it removes unnecessary steps and brings changes to the workers' attitudes. So adapting the 5S process for managing a project means reducing project delay and increasing workplace safety.

Implementing the 5S process can be very cheap for some cases, but implementing it in large scale organization level requires capital investment. For managing and implementing the 5S process successfully, the following three things are a must.

1. Commitment

As a manager, you and the rest of the management team should be committed towards implementing all five steps of the 5S process. You should also get the required resources for implementing all the five S's and ensure the discipline of your team to sustain the implemented change.

2. Support from the Top

Implementing the 5S process is not only about changing the working attitude of your subordinates but also about the changing the mindset of the top management. For implementing the 5S process in all organizational levels, you require investments, time, and resources. For all of this, you need to have the confidence of senior management.

3. Measure the Change

You need to constantly monitor and measure your team's performance for two reasons: By measuring performance you can be sure that the working habits of your team are not really drifting back to their old practices, and you can use statistics documenting your team's improvement to gain the confidence of senior management for implementing the 5S process on a larger scale.

The 5S process is a Japanese method useful for achieving a neater, cleaner work environment which, in turn, improves productivity. Successful implementation of the 5S process is a combination of a physical environment change and working attitude changes. Hence, it requires a whole-hearted commitment and strong support from the top.

Chapter 8: How to Document a 5s Project

Some project managers should first look at implementing 5S in stages. For example, teams would be trained in Sort, before moving on to Set in Order and so on. The principle here is before you can document and sustain your 5S project, the entire organization and teams have to understand the processes fully.

Yet somehow, even if your team understands the 5S Methodology, you have to be able to evaluate it, analyze it, and audit it, so what tools should you use?

Tools to Document 5S Projects

In 5S, there are many forms and tools that are used, including red-tags, labelling, colour-coding for ease of use in inventory, bins, must-do signs, and safety warnings. For projects, however, these tools must be converted into tools that will work for the entire team.

Here are some good examples of the tools you should implement in your 5S projects:

1. **Change Control:** Initially, you will need a good change control plan and learn how to deal with change resistance, especially when switching to a methodology this rigid.
2. **Meetings:** Because every team member in 5S is allowed to offer suggestions, it is essential

that you hold regular meetings and identify areas that need to be improved upon.

3. **Kaizen Tools:** These are great for evaluating your 5S project and include PDCA or Plan, Do, Check, and Act. With the PDCA method, you can quickly identify areas that need improvement and then immediately act upon them.

4. **Audits:** 5S audits are also needed at regular intervals.

5. **Step Processes:** Each one of the 5S processes should be written and detailed and made available to all team members working on the project.

6. **System and Space Evaluation:** Before implementing 5S into your projects, you need to evaluate your systems and workspace environments.

   a. Are the systems you utilize in order?

   b. Are workspace areas in places where collaborative teams have access to one another?

   c. Do you have a centralized place where team members can obtain various tools without delays?

7. **Checklists:** 5S checklists are also essential.

Chapter 9: 5s or 6s Methodology

Somewhere along the line a few United States manufacturers have decided the 5S Methodology needs another element -safety. Proponents of the 5S method contend that safety is already an element so why fix what is not broken? In this chapter we take a look at adding the safety step making it 6S.

The premise behind 5S is that order and repetitiveness of processes produces quick outcomes, especially when combined with the Just-In-Time (JIT) inventory process. Should here be a debate about 5S vs. 6S or are companies using the 5S process happy with the way it is?

America's Choice

1913 Ford Assembly Line While the sixth element, "safety," doesn't appear on the 5S list; many companies argue the safety issue isn't needed because the steps and processes ensure safety as a key factor, so why change it?

If the fifth S of the 5S Methodology utilizes sustainability allowing for safe manufacturing processes, why reinvent the wheel or is this a choice made by American companies?

In 1992, a report released by the U.S. Bureau of Labour Statistics by Richard Wokutch and Josetta McLaughlin called "The U.S. and Japanese Work

Injury and Illness Experience" offered some surprising statistics.

Japan does seem to take order and efficiency seriously and found "Japanese systems for regulating and managing occupational safety and health in these plans are superior to the United States." Also according to this report, Japan auto manufacturing plants located in America "have higher incidences of cumulative trauma" when compared to U.S.-owned auto plants due to the "faster pace of production and more strictly defined work motions."

It would seem from these statistics that safety may be a needed element in American factories. By adding the sixth S, or safety, workplace accidents and injuries may be swayed in the U.S.

Which Is Better?

6S US Sign When it comes to 5S vs. 6S, one must also consider the use of the Kaizen Principle, a continuous process improvement process closely associated with companies utilizing the 5S Methodology to reduce defects and focus on quality.

Workplace injuries and workman's compensation claims are higher in the United States than in Japan and if one looks at how widely the 5S Methodology is utilized in Japan, is this the reason American companies will only be able to use 5S if it becomes 6S and adds the safety element?

Certainly, the United States Occupational Safety and Health Organization (OSHA) has made safety an important issue whereby employers must comply with rules on safety including safety manuals, meetings, and required Material Data Safety Sheets (MSDS).

In Japan, injury and illness statistics are gathered by the Ministry of Labour and subsequently reported to the Labour of Standards Bureau, which helps to set required safety elements on the jobsite. In America, on the other hand, there is not only just OSHA compliance, but state workman's compensation reporting, Bureau of Labour reporting and, in some cases, the Equal Employment Opportunity Commission (EEOC) which does investigate complaints of some on-the-job injury complaints not reported in other words, maybe too many cooks in the kitchen compared to Japan.

When it comes to using the 5S Methodology and adding another "S" or the safety factor, perhaps it depends on how well the methodology is utilized and followed. 5S requires a commitment from the lowest-in-rank to the highest-in-rank employee and members of upper management in order for the methodology to succeed and it does seem the "sustain" process includes attention to safety.

Considering those too many cooks in the kitchen in the United States, perhaps those manufacturing plants wishing to implement 5S should consider 6S at least initially until the process is uniform, accepted, and understood by every worker, supervisor, and management within these plants.

So, which is best 5S vs. 6S?

Here, the long-term and established practices of 5S may be the key in determining the best solution. Companies new to 5S may consider adding the safety issue until safety factors and how to handle them can be included in the fifth element of 5S or the sustainment policies and procedures.

Chapter 10: Sample of a 5s Mission Statement

Perhaps 5S is the most efficient way to run an operation whether it is for a product, project or process, but before you begin your exploration into the 5S Methodology, do you need a mission statement? In this chapter we will look at samples of a mission statement for 5S, no matter what the goal.

The 5S Methodology uses sort of the same in concept. If things are organized, structured, planned for, kept orderly, and clean, it's easier to get the job done. Utilized first in Japan by Toyota, 5S has been sweeping the world of manufacturing but it can be used in projects or processes as well.

To implement the 5S Methodology, just like any other project management methodology, you must have a vision and a sample of a mission statement for 5S. When writing your 5S mission statement, keep in mind that vision and mission statements are two different things. Your vision is the "what" you want to do and the mission is the "how" you will complete that vision, or how you will entice customers that they need what you have to sell.

A 5S Company Finds Their Mission

One family-owned Internet store, the 5 S Store wanted to offer 5S tools such as bins, storage racks, tools, labels, posters, and 5S safety items to companies who wanted to go 5S. They admitted after dreaming up their vision statement, they forgot the mission and began ordering inventory from many vendors incurring large shipping costs and lots of inventory with no organized place to store it.

The family sat back and came up with this mission statement; "To provide high quality products and superior service to individuals looking to implement 5S organization throughout their facility." With this mission, they were able to complete their own vision by organizing and readjusting their ordering and inventory problems to a more streamlined process, thus enabling quick delivery on orders. But what about your product, project or process? What is a good sample of a mission statement for 5S?

Creating Your Own Mission Statement

Let's take a look at sample mission statements for 5S in the following areas; product or project:

Product

Sort of conjoined with manufacturing, if you have a widget that is different than any other widget out there, that's your vision, but how will you sell it? Now you need a mission. Say your new widget is a machine that helps people set timers in their entire homes so they can skip small tasks upon waking such as watering the garden, making the coffee, feeding the dog or recording their favourite TV show.

You already know you have a fantastic machine that will save time but how will you sell that idea? Consider this mission statement: "To aid people everywhere in streamlining morning tasks through 5S automation with a goal to get them out the door with a touch of a button." That's certainly enticing and by utilizing the 5S Methodology to build your widget machine, you can keep costs reasonable and efficiency high.

Project

Say your boss sends you to the "land of nowhere," the messy storage room, and your job is to clean and organize it. Well, here your boss claimed the vision, but what mission will you use to complete the project? First you might take a look at your organization and what it does and needs from that storage room. "To create an interactive storage space where inventory and supplies are available on demand through a 5S process that is constantly maintained." Wow, your boss would be proud of that sample mission statement for a 5S project.

By utilizing the 5 steps in 5S, Sort, Set in Order, Shine, Standardize, and Sustain, your project will be complete in no time and integrated through the usage of the 5S Methodology.

Creating a 5S Mission Statement for a Process

With the 5S Methodology, you can also create a sample mission statement for 5S with regard to a process:

Process

Say you are a used car dealer and you need a better process to get the customer from the salesperson to the finance director to the delivery process. In the past, your process fails miserably because no one is organized or ready when called upon. When it's time for Andy the salesperson to pass the customer to Becky the finance director, she is out to lunch. When Becky is ready to pass on the customer to Rob the delivery guy, he is already gone home for the day. Let's face it, your delivery process is a mess.

Why not start with a mission that says, "To ensure each customer experiences a standardized delivery process that is swift, organized, and orderly with an emphasis on customer satisfaction." That is a great mission statement, but now you need to utilize 5S in your delivery process. Here is the great part of the 5S Methodology. Again by using the 5 steps in 5S you can determine via shifts of personnel who will work as a team in an orderly and efficient fashion to ensure that no customer is left standing or waiting.

Do You Really Need a 5S Mission Statement?

I have seen and written many mission statements in my time as a business owner. Some were for companies, others were for departments. The answer to the question do you need a sample of a vision statement for 5S is yes.

If you expect to implement 5S into your product, project or process, first you must have the all-important sell or idea on how you want to deliver your 5S product or service. If you can't explain why your "how" idea is a good idea, you will never get to the 5S Methodology process; you will never implement anything that even resembles it.

Every streamlined, efficient management methodology consists of explaining and understanding the mission or the how first and then moving on to the nuts and bolts or detail of that how. I visited a car dealer we worked with couple of years ago just to see how they are sustaining the 5S program we put into the company. The Chief Executive officer said "In my business as a car dealer, I try to be Agile. I want processes to be short so customers don't have to wait. While the 5S Methodology would work just as well, I may use a Vision statement that says "To become synonymous with driving in England." My sample mission statement for a 5S might be, "To ensure every customer who enters our dealership has a fast, accurate, and acceptable buying experience that meets every car need they have before they leave the store." Now that's something I might work on!

Chapter 11: Working Through a Sample 5s Check Sheet

Part of using the 5S Methodology developed by Toyota Motor Corporation is utilizing 5S check sheets. In this chapter we will explain the concept and how to ensure your projects run smoothly.

These housekeeping words set the guidelines for the 5S Methodology, especially when considering utilizing the methodology to improve or streamline workplace or project processes. Everyone has a co-worker with an office that is a mess, nothing can be found and they are totally unorganized.

With 5S, organization is key in successful operations. Along with streamlined processes comes the need for monitoring and the use of a 5S check sheet.

The 5S Monitoring Process

The 5S check list is a way to audit and sustain organized processes within production. The auditing or monitoring process is necessary in 5S as it pertains to standardizing and sustaining. A good 5S check sheet grades each housekeeping area to help ensure the process stays organized.

What is included in the 5S Audit Check List?

Because the 5S Methodology relies on organized, standard practices and processes to improve and sustain quality in production, the 5S check sheet divides each of the housekeeping stages that are graded from zero to five; zero being unacceptable and four as outstanding or perfect.

A substandard 5S process would show a much lower score, however, because the 5S audit check quickly identifies the areas that need improvement, the 5S auditor can pass on the information to the 5S leader, usually top management.

Upon receipt of the 5S audit check sheet, the leaders of the process are then able to determine if additional steps, tools or methods are needed to sustain the production process.

The Importance of a 5S Audit

The 5S process depends upon constant monitoring and evaluating much like Six Sigma or Lean Six Sigma. An important part of the 5S audit is the ability for the auditors to red tag certain items that are unacceptable or substandard.

Once red tagged items are corrected, a continual 5S audit check sheet will not only show improvement but 5S leaders will actually be able to see the improved production process, unlike some other quality improvement methodologies that utilize more intense methods of analyzing quality.

Chapter 12: When and How to Use Kaizen Events

Many organizations are reluctant to utilize kaizen events because such events take a team of employees away from their "real jobs" for three to five days at a time. Companies often choose to substitute kaizen events with projects assigned to one or two individuals. Because of a lack of perceived importance and a lack of substantial participation and buy-in, very rarely does this result in true improvement. In fact, it often results in organizations claiming that lean does not work for them.

When I encounter companies in this situation, I argue that the effects of a properly planned and executed kaizen event will pay for the perceived "lost time" of the participants many times over. In fact, their "real jobs" will become easier because they will include less "fire fighting" and more productive activities since kaizen events will address many of the day-to-day problems with permanent solutions instead of Band-Aids.

Kaizen events are focused three to five days breakthrough events that generally include the following activities:
1. Training
2. Defining the problem/goals
3. Documenting the current state
4. Brainstorming and developing a future state
5. Implementation

6. Developing a follow-up plan
7. Presenting results
8. Celebrating successes

This process works in a variety of situations to solve a variety of problems. Kaizen events are often planned using value stream mapping to target the right areas for improvement. What follows is a list of some of the problems that can be solved using kaizen events:

Decreasing changeover time on a piece of equipment or process. Using kaizen, a team can improve upon the time to change over equipment using the SMED system, developed by Shigeo Shingo.
1. Organizing the workplace using 5S.
2. Creating a one-piece-flow work cell.
3. Developing a pull system.
4. Improving equipment reliability through TPM (Total Productive Maintenance).
5. Improving the manufacturability of a product design.
6. Improving a product development process.
7. Improving other administrative processes such as order processing, procurement, engineering change processing and other paperwork/information processing activities.

Kaizen events, however, cannot solve any problem within an organization. There are certain types of improvements for which other methods should be used. Process improvements (such as Six Sigma-type analyses) aimed at yield improvement and variation/scrap reduction are key examples. Suppose that a particular process has a first-pass yield of only

85 percent when it would need to be much closer to 100 percent to run in a one-piece-flow environment. If the process must be analyzed using experiments and statistical methods, it would make sense to utilize a team but not a kaizen event. To implement these types of improvements, a problem-solving team (or a Six Sigma team) that meets regularly over a period of time works better than a kaizen team meeting for five consecutive days.

In order to utilize kaizen events effectively, it is important to understand the types of problems for which kaizen events should and should not be used. With proper planning, kaizen events can bring breakthrough improvement to an organization on its lean journey.

Chapter 13: 5s Implementation

Put simply, 5S is method of creating, maintaining and improving a clean and orderly workplace that exposes waste and errors. 5S helps identify unplanned levels of inventory either as tools, materials, work in progress or finished goods. Often we can use simple visual processes to help us identify these problems quickly through systems that provide instruction, information and feedback on how well the operational process is working. 5S can be applied to any physical process in the factory and in the office.

5S is much more than just "housekeeping". Housekeeping and an organised workplace are the results of 5S, but the real purpose of 5S is to make problems more evident more quickly.

5S is a great place to start on our Lean initiative because it promotes an action oriented approach to change and allows people at all levels in the business to get involved and provide input with improving their workplace.

Here are some suggestions for implementing 5S

Create a sense of urgency around your 5S activities. Let's understand you are implementing 5S in your business and why you need to do this now and why you shouldn't leave it for 12 months. If 5S does not improve your operation and fix people's frustrations why would you use it?

Have the senior management team develop a vision for how the business will be different once 5S has been implemented across the organisation. Take the time to put some thought into how it will affect your Value Streams and the expected operational benefits that will result.

Implement in a pilot area first and then develop and execute the rollout plan for the rest of the organisation. The rollout plan should include regular and achievable milestones and targets that are visible and unambiguous. Each area should have visual 5S measures displayed in the work area, and celebrate the achievement of their targets at least every few months.

Make sure 5S is seen in the context of the whole Lean initiative and not as a standalone tool, and make sure people know why you are doing 5S.

Make sure that your 5S activities are "successful". That means making sure that people actually solve some of their problems with the application of 5S. Think about ways to set people up for success.

Don't just implement 5S because it is easy; implement 5S to engage people in improving the flow of work and eliminating waste. If you cannot clearly see how 5S is going to improve the operation, chose another tool that will drive real improvement first.

Plan for training and coaching of staff: You should not expect people to understand 5S without relevant training. Think about ways to standardise the 5S training so that everyone receives the same information. The training can be structured into the kaizen blitz's that are planned for each area.

Insist that management lead by example by getting involved with 5S activities on the floor and implementing 5S in their own work areas. Every time a manager condones or ignores a 5S issue that should be addressed we are eroding the whole program because it shows that we are not serious. What is not said is often more powerful than what is said. Build 5S reviews into management Gemba walks.

Build 5S standard work into our processes and daily activities at all levels in the business. Don't allow 5S to be something that we do only when we have spare time, or on a Friday afternoon. We don't approach Health and Safety this way.

Through the involvement of the team members in the work area, clearly define the expected 5S standards in all work areas and use visual standards to display and monitor these expectations.

Take the time to have the team members visit good examples of 5S in other parts of your organisation or outside the company.

Use structured problem solving techniques with the teams to solve specific 5S issues. Use of a standard process will accelerate the uptake of the tools as people get more practice with the techniques.

Ensure that all work instructions reflect the 5S requirements for all activities and tasks, particularly for putting away materials, tools and product.

Take every opportunity to emphasise 5S by including it in all job descriptions and every meeting. If you apply the same principles to the implementation of 5S as you have to Health and Safety then you are more likely to succeed.

Build 5S expectations into your performance measures, but ensure that audits and measures are designed to help people understand why you are doing 5S. Sustainable results will not be realised if people are just finding ways to improve audit scores without fully understanding the real objectives of 5S.

Have the Leadership Team review progress on a regular basis and continue to set new targets. As the new behaviours become habits, develop ways to continuously improve the 5S culture. Consider rewarding and recognising teams for their level of improvement or innovative solutions to 5S issues.

Be innovative about how 5S can be applied to other processes in other parts of the organisation. Every organisational process will benefit from 5S thinking.

Chapter 14: Philosophy of 5S

Do you want to be the slave of your working environment, or its master?

Do you want your working area to help you to do your job, or to hinder your efforts?

Do you want to be rushing to complete your tasks, or have time to take pride in them?

5S is a Workplace Organisation system that enables you to be the master of your work area, a work area that helps you to do your job instead of hindering you, so that you have time to take pride in your efforts. It is there to enable you to get each activity right the first time, every time.

Don't get caught up in the message that 5S is a discipline of managers over workers. If you have been taught that, then the teacher didn't know what they were talking about.

5S involves everyone, from directors to the guy who sweeps the floor. It benefits everyone. It depends on everyone.

For the system to work, no-one can hide. Everyone has to be involved, everyone has to contribute.

Every work area should be a shop window to show off the benefits of 5S. Factory shop floors that are untidy, dirty and disorganised have to go. Managers' offices that are disorganised, filled with filing cabinets that contain nothing of worth, these have to go. Director's offices with files lining the walls that contain irrelevant information from years past have to go.

Who should clean the factory floor? The people who work there. Everyone accepts that.

So who should clean the director's offices? The directors. Managers should clean their own offices.

You did be surprised how clean and tidy areas are kept when the user is responsible for cleaning them.

If you are a director or manager looking to introduce 5S, you need to start thinking like a Royal Marine where the men have to complete a forced march in a certain time with a certain weight in their backpack. The officers have to complete in a faster time. In the famed obstacle course the officers must complete the course faster than the men.

If you are a director or manager introducing 5S, you need to be better than the standard you expect from your reports. Don't do it to them do it with them! Set an example. A director or manager implementing 5S must accept this. If you report into a director or manger you must expect it.

Chapter 15: Sustain the Gains of Lean Improvements

Many organizations make some early 5S improvements and then slide back into their old ways of doing things. Other organizations continue to maintain their 5S programs for many years.

What separates a successful 5S program from one that is headed for failure?

An unsuccessful implementation of 5S was never a complete 5S implementation. The fifth "S" stands for "sustain;" if implemented completely, a 5S program will have longevity. There are four keys to successfully sustaining 5S: commitment, top management support and performance measurement.

1. Commitment

The first key is to commit to all five S's. While this may appear to be obvious, I once had a conversation with a well-meaning executive who told me: "We are just going to implement 3S for now. We aren't ready for all five." The fifth S, "shitsuke" in Japanese, actually translates more closely to "commitment" than "sustain." shitsuke' is a typical teaching and attitude toward any undertaking to inspire pride and adherence to the standards established." If your entire organization is not committed to 5S, your organization's 5S program will be short-lived.

2. Top Management Support

The first and second keys go hand-in-hand. Commitment is not possible without top management's visible support for the program. All employees must believe that the organization has committed to the program. One way to encourage top management to get involved on a continuing basis is for them to conduct quarterly 5S visits in which executives inspect each work area to 5S conditions and offer advice and support to the employees. Another effective method for demonstrating top management support is for executives to mandate and participate in visible promotion of 5S. Some ways to promote 5S include:

Designated 5S days: Select a day per month or per quarter to emphasize 5S throughout the plant.

Slogans: Select a 5S related slogan, post it in public areas throughout the plant, pass out shirts made up with the slogan to successful 5S teams, etc.

Public announcements: In monthly or quarterly announcements/all-employee meetings, take some time to emphasize the importance of 5S.

Seminars: Have employees participate in seminars throughout the year. Some of these should be 5S related.

3. Performance Measurement and Reward System

The third key is to measure 5S performance in each work area and set up a reward system to reward teams that achieve 5S success. Organizations that have successful 5S programs measure their performance through weekly audits using checklists and score sheets. Results of the audits are posted in public areas. This creates an atmosphere of friendly competition and will help to instil pride in the teams you have set up. This measurement and competition should be combined with a reward system; most successful organizations offer monthly or quarterly rewards for their teams in various 5S categories. The rewards can range from movie tickets to cash bonuses.

These three keys are simple but powerful. Your organization must commit to all five of the five pillars. Top management must show visible support for the program. And, your organization must set up a 5S performance measurement and reward system.

4. Visual Workplace

If your company uses lean practices to improve plant operations and business performance, or if you are considering a lean transformation, you are not alone. In recent years, more companies have adopted lean as a continuous improvement method to improve profitability, enhance customer satisfaction and maintain a competitive edge in the marketplace.

Within lean practices is a growing concept called "visual workplace," also known as visual factory or visual management, and it's a critical part of any lean initiative. Visual workplace helps sustain lean operations by using visual tools to ensure that improvements remain clearly visible, readily understood and consistently adhered to long after the lean event is over.

Opportunities to Reduce Waste

Businesses are often surprised to learn that only a small fraction of their activities actually add value for their customers. In a lean workplace, "waste" is any activity that adds no value for a customer. It's not uncommon that 50 percent or more of a facility's activities are considered waste.

A primary cause of waste is information deficits; employees simply lack the knowledge they need to do their jobs efficiently and effectively. They may not fully understand their priorities or deadlines, nor the proper way to perform tasks. This leads employees to waste valuable time and motion searching, asking, waiting, retrieving, reworking or just plain giving up.

A visual workplace is self-explanatory. It displays information that is visible at a glance and at the point of use, eliminates questions and ensures that best practices are followed. By clearly displaying information such as instructions, warnings, standards and other critical operations knowledge, visual tools help to properly guide employee actions. These tools also make it easier to detect abnormalities in products, equipment and processes, and provide workers with real-time feedback on where they stand against goals and expectations.

We implemented an effective visual system at client companies in year 2011 which has resulted in the following dramatic improvements:

1. 15 percent increase in throughput
2. 70 percent cut in materials handling
3. 60 percent decrease in floor space
4. 80 percent decrease in flow distance
5. 68 percent reduction in rack storage
6. 50 percent decrease in annual physical inventory time
7. 96 percent decrease in defects

Clearly, visual workplace plays a key role in creating the empowered, creative and aligned work culture that is the end goal of any lean transformation.

Visuality Encompasses All Lean Concepts

Visual workplace techniques represent a critical component of lean concepts, including 5S, standard work, Total Productive Maintenance (TPM), just-in-time (JIT) inventory management and kanban-based pull production. Here are some ideas on how visual devices can be put to profitable use in your lean initiatives.

5S workplace organization: This technique focuses on sorting, cleaning and organizing to set the foundation for a stable work environment. Visual devices help maintain long-term visual order by clearly identifying aisles, storage areas and locations for equipment, tools, parts and products. Visuals such as bin markers, floor marking tapes, shadow boards and tool ID labels ensure that items are consistently returned to their proper place, eliminating wasted search and retrieval time.

Standard work and quick changeover: Visual tools ensure that workers readily understand proper setup, operating and inspection procedures. Instead of just storing information in binders and computer drives, post critical information clearly right at the point of use. In mixed work environments, use colour-coding to identify the proper parts and tools for the job at hand. You will simplify training, prevent mistakes, reduce cycle times and improve safety.

Total Productive Maintenance: Identifying abnormalities at a glance is a key objective of TPM. Once equipment has been centre-lined, visual devices such as multi-colour gauge labels and oil level indicators can clearly indicate when operating conditions are out of spec. Visual devices also help machine operators perform autonomous maintenance tasks by clearly identifying preventive maintenance (PM) points and indicating the correct use of grease and lubricants.

JIT and kanban: A key goal of lean is to eliminate excess inventory. The concepts of just-in-time inventory management and kanban-based pull production help achieve these goals by ensuring that product is produced only in the time and amount needed. Visual reorder indicators control stocking levels for inventory, and kanban cards are used to prevent excess production.

Lean metrics and management: Open communication is a hallmark of a lean business. Employees need to know what is expected of them and how they are performing. Visual displays such as scoreboards, scheduling charts, team communication boards and recognition displays all help to keep information flowing between employees, work, departments and upper management.

Whichever lean tools you use, visual thinking can reinforce and sustain improvements throughout your plant. There is much to be gained by creating a workplace where employees are guided by visual information that tells them at a glance what to do, how to do it properly, and where to quickly find what they need. The accompanying boost in productivity, quality, capacity, on-time delivery and equipment reliability will make your facility leaner than ever.

Chapter 16: Conclusion

5S, or the five pillars of the visual workplace, is a systematic process of workplace organization. When I ask manufacturing people about the components of 5S, most of them don't think they are relevant.

"That's just a system of keeping things organized and clean, right? Oh yeah, and they have this crazy idea that toolboxes are bad." Or, sometimes I hear; "Why make a big program out of cleaning up?"

5S is not simply eliminating toolboxes and cleaning up. While the concepts are easy to understand, most companies have not implemented them. Implementation of 5S has many benefits; higher quality, lower costs, reliable deliveries and improved safety to name a few. These benefits are clearly relevant to any manufacturer, and they are not had simply by eliminating toolboxes and cleaning up.

The intent of 5S is to have only what you need available in the workplace, a designated place for everything, a standard way of doing things and the discipline to maintain it. Created in Japan, the components of 5S are: seiri, seiton, seiso, seiketsu and shitsuke. Translated to English, we have:

Sort: Remove all items from the workplace that are not needed for current production.

Set in order: Arrange needed items so that they are easy to find and put away. Items used often are placed closer to the employee.

Shine: Make sure everything is clean, functioning and ready to go.

Standardize: This is the method you use to maintain the first three S's.

Sustain: Make a habit of properly maintaining correct procedures.

For the organization, this creates fewer defects, less waste, fewer delays, fewer injuries and fewer breakdowns. These advantages translate to lower cost and higher quality.

For the operator, the components of 5S create a superior working environment. They give the operator an opportunity to provide creative input regarding how the workplace should be organized and laid out and how standard work should be done. Operators will be able to find things easily, every time. The workplace will be cleaner and safer. Jobs will be simpler and more satisfying with many obstacles and frustrations removed.

Just to re-cap on what we already know and talk about in the earlier chapters of this book.

The first "S" (Sort) requires you to distinguish between what is needed and what is not needed. Then, it requires you to discard what is not needed. This is known as "red-tagging." A team goes through all items (tools, equipment, material, etc.) and asks the question: "Do I need this to do my job on a regular basis?" Items that are used very infrequently or not used should be red-tagged. After determining what is actually needed, update all documentation to reflect the needed parts.

The second "S" (Set in Order) requires you to organize things so that they are easy to use, and label them so that anyone can find, use and return them to the correct place easily. Visual controls should be used where practicable in this activity; a visual control is any communication device used in the work environment that tells you at a glance how work should be done. The requirements for setting in order include.

Equipment and tool organization:
1. Simple, organized storage with visual confirmation (you know exactly where it goes and if it is missing/empty with just a glance).
2. Tools and equipment used most frequently are closest to employee.
3. Workstations have a place for each tool, with no toolboxes or drawers that interfere with visibility and require unneeded motion to open and close.
4. Taping: Tape the floor to indicate areas of operations, parts, walkways, discrepant material and hazards.
5. Work instructions: Make sure these are current and at the workstation.

Signboard strategy:
1. Indicate cell, product lines and workstations.
2. Indicate production goals and status.

3. Post area information boards with key status indicators (inventory, training, calibration etc).

Ergonomics:
1. Follow ergonomic guidelines in work/tool design.

The third "S" (Shine) involves bringing the workspace back to proper order by the end of each day. It requires periodic (at least once daily) cleanup, responsible person(s) identified for cleanup, establishment of cleanup/restocking methods (tools, checklists, etc.), and periodic supervisor inspection.

The fourth "S" (Standardize) is the method by which you maintain the first three S's. Organization, orderliness and cleanliness are maintained and made habitual by instituting 3S duties into regular work routines. The methods need to be standardized and required company-wide.

The fifth "S" (Sustain) allows the organization to sustain its 5S program. This requires:
1. An executive 5S champion to ensure that 5S becomes part of the culture;
2. Periodic walk-through inspections/audits with posted results; and,
3. 5S performance measurement of workgroups.

Implementation of this final "S" is where most companies fall back into their old ways of doing things. Very often, 5S is thought of as an activity rather than an element of company culture. Companies implement 5S for several months only to find themselves back to their previous state. To make 5S work, it is critical that performance be measured and that top management is committed.

Keep improving!!

Resource and References

Shigeo Shingo, Norman Bodek, Collin McLoughlin: Kaizen and the Art of Creative Thinking - The Scientific Thinking Mechanism

Shigeo Shingo; Fundamental Principles of Lean Manufacturing

Shigeo Shingo, Andrew P. Dillon (Translator); Zero Quality Control: Source Inspection and the Poka-yoke System

Shigeo Shingo; Non-Stock Production: The Shingo System of Continuous Improvement

Shigeo Shingo; A Study of the Toyota Production System from an Industrial Engineering Viewpoint

Shigeo Shingo; A Study of the Toyota Production System from an Industrial Engineering Viewpoint

Drucker, P. (1993) Post-Capitalist Society

Drucker, P., "What Makes an Effective Executive", Harvard Business review, June 2004

Lessons from Toyota's long drive, an interview with Katsuaki Watanabe, HBR, July 2007

Liker, J. & D. Meier, Toyota Talent, McGraw Hill, 2007

Shook, J. , Managing To Learn, Lean Enterprise Institute 2008

Fishman, C., "No Satisfaction", Fast Company, Dec 2006/Jan 2007

Womack, J. & J. Shook, Lean Management and The Role of Lean Leadership, Lean Enterprise Institute presentation, Oct. 2006

www.ingramcontent.com/pod-product-compliance
Lightning Source LLC
Chambersburg PA
CBHW071747170526
45167CB00003B/972